REALITY

AND THE

GOOD

REALITY

AND THE

GOOD

Josef Pieper

translated by

Stella Lange

Henry Regnery Company
Chicago

First published in German as *Die Wirklichkeit Und Das Gute*

7th edition – 1963

Library of Congress Catalogue Card Number 67-28494

Manufactured in the United States of America

"A wise man is one who savors all things as they really are."

Bernard of Clairvaux

"In our doing and acting everything depends on this, that we comprehend objects clearly and treat them according to their nature."

Goethe

Contents

Introduction

The Thesis

All obligation is based upon being. Reality is the foundation of ethics. The good is that which is in accord with reality.

He who wishes to know and to do the good must turn his gaze upon the objective world of being. Not upon his own "ideas," not upon his "conscience," not upon "values," not upon arbitrarily established "ideals" and "models." He must turn away from his own act and fix his eyes upon reality.

"Reality" means two things. This twofold meaning is expressed by the two Latin words *realis* and *actualis;* the one is derived from *res*—thing, the other from *actus*—action.

Res is everything that is "presented" to our sense perception or our intellectual cognition; all that has being independently of our thinking. "Real" in this sense is whatever is "opposed" to us. Here the original meaning of the word "object" is revealed and confirmed. Not-real is that which is merely thought (but its being thought is also something real); scholastic philosophy gave it the name *ens rationis*, "a thing of thought." Reality (in the sense of *realis*) is the whole of being which is independent of thought. When St. Thomas wishes to designate this "reality" —not its fullness of content but its objectivity, which is antecedent to all cognition—then he uses the word "*res*" (which Theodor Haecker calls a "core-word of the Latin language" which "the Romans gave to the whole world").

The second sense of "reality" indicates the contrast not to what is merely thought but to what is merely potential—though this potentiality is also "real." The *ens in actu* is opposed not to the *ens rationis* but to the *ens in potentia*. Reality in this sense means the realized potentiality.

The statement that reality is the basis of the good is quite applicable to both meanings of "real." But in our subsequent discussion it shall be considered primarily and for the most part from the point of view of the first meaning.

According to the second and equally important meaning, the statement would signify this: to be good means to be directed toward realization. This direction toward realization must be understood primarily as the will to self-realization: "Every being is perfect insofar as it is realized, and imperfection lies in this, that its potentiality is not realized."[1]

But to be directed toward realization means also to be directed in accordance with the inherent direction of the potentiality of all things; it means an affirmation of all created being, "love" for all that is; it means desiring for and granting to every being its peculiar form of realization. All this must be thought of as completely free from any philanthropic self-complacent sentimentality. But ultimately and primarily this affirmative direction toward realization includes the direction toward God himself, who is the *Ens Actualissimum*, that being which is absolutely realized from the very beginning, in which all potentiality is completely realized in action. The affirmation of this supreme reality by man contains within itself, both as source and as summation, all modes of direction toward self-realization and all possibilities of the affirmation of that which is.[2] But this meaning of the thesis shall be touched upon only incidentally in this treatise.

Reality is the basis of the good. This means for our present purpose, according to the meaning of "real—*realis*," that to be good is to do justice to objective being; that is good which corresponds to "the thing"; the good is that which is in accord with objective reality.

There is a statement of Goethe, "All laws and and moral principles may be reduced to one—the truth."[3] But truth is the revelation of reality. Truth is the "proclamation of being," says Hilary,[4] and Augustine says, "Truth is that which manifests what is."[5] So he who undertakes to reduce morality to truth, and, following this arrow, probes more deeply, beyond "truth" or rather through it, necessarily reaches being. All laws and moral principles may be reduced to reality.

The good lies indeed in the proper relation of action to the reason which truly understands, and so evil is indeed a kind of "logical" contradiction. But reason is nothing but the "passage" to reality. And he who attempts to survey at one glance this circuit, reality-understanding-action, and to express it in one word, will find that evil ultimately proves to be an "ontic" contradiction, a contradiction of being, something that opposes reality, that does not correspond to "the thing."

This makes it plain how much depends, when we are establishing a basis for ethics, on whether we start from a realistic theory of cognition or from one which—as Goethe says of Kant's—does not reach the object."[6]

An insight into the nature of the good as rooted in objective being, of itself compels us to carry it out in a definite human attitude, and it makes certain attitudes impossible.

It makes impossible the attitude of always referring to oneself and to the judgment of one's conscience, which is considered as providing the norm in each instance. We are forced now to look through and beyond our own moral judgment to the norm presented to us by the objective reality of being. When one is seeking his way, do his eyes and his glances strive for anything but this: to note the objects themselves as landmarks or hindrances and to make them yield him information? Thus, the man who wishes to realize the good does not look upon his own act but upon the truth of real objects.

"Objectivity," if thereby we mean "fidelity to being," is the proper attitude of man.

But we must note that man himself of course also belongs to the "objective reality of being," as an object to himself.

In the preceding pages we have formulated in outline the thesis which shall be explained and established in what follows. The explanation will be based upon the work of St. Thomas Aquinas. However, we scarcely need to say that the purpose of this reliance upon the great doctor of the Church in our comments and explanations is not "historical."

A Realistic Theory of Cognition and Intellectualistic Ethics

The correctness of our thesis depends on two conditions: first, the condition that our cognition attains the truth of real things, that it "reaches the object." "The cognitive spirit advances into the essence of the thing."[1] Second, the condition that our willing and acting are determined by knowledge: "The will is not the first norm; it is guided by knowledge; not only in us, but also in God."[2] Before and above the will stands the cognitive relation to reality. The good is essentially dependent upon and interiorly penetrated by knowledge. This is always and everywhere valid, even in the case of the so-called purely "voluntaristic" action; even for willing which is objectively evil. Even the man who denies that our willing and acting are determined by knowledge is in his action dependent upon that which he thinks he knows; and all evil rests in some way upon an error, upon a supposed knowledge.[3] He is good "who does the truth" (*John* 3:21). "The good, then, presupposes the true."[4] "The good, as truth, is related more primarily to knowledge than it is related, as good, to the will."[5] Virtue is "the seal of the cognitive power impressed upon the will."[6] The cognitive power is "the root of all virtue."[7] In one word: "The good of man lies in being according to reason, his evil in being against reason."[8]

The possibility of contemporary misunderstanding in regard to this ethical "intellectualism" compels us to certain explanations.

First of all, we must not overlook the fact that

"reason" here not only includes but means the essential relation to reality. It is nothing else than the power of man to take into himself the truth of real things. The original meaning of the German word for reason (*Vernunft*—perception)* here keeps its full force, and "reason"—perception—here signifies not so much the "process of cognition" as "that which is perceived."

Furthermore, the intellectualism of St. Thomas Aquinas—and of all Christian philosophy—must not be understood to mean that the whole realm of human action is, or can be, made clear by the light of mere human knowledge. This complete clarification is not even a true human aim or end, since in itself it transcends the power of a created spirit; man cannot know himself completely because he is not his own cause. "The first act of the will does not result from the command of reason"[9]; the roots and origins of the human will do not lie in the bright field of man's own knowledge, but in the dark zone of instinctive urges or of a higher power.[10] Of course this darkness is not wholly impenetrable, but it is so for man; the "irrational" source of the human will is illumined by the divine knowledge. However, its light is "unapproachable" for the creature (1 *Tim.* 6:16). Nevertheless, with regard to the sphere of free and responsible action, it remains true: The good for man lies in being in accord with reason.[11]

---

*Translator's note: We might compare here the use of the word "sensible" for "reasonable" in common English parlance.

This combination of a realistic theory of cognition and an "intellectualistic" ethics is the basis of all arguments for the thesis that the good is that which is in accord with reality. It is also the basis for the organization of the developing proof of this thesis. Section I will deal with the manner in which knowledge is related to the objective reality of being, section II with the way in which the will is molded by the cognition of reality.

Section I

Reality as the Measure of Cognition

A basic principle of any realist epistemology is this: "Objects are the measure of our knowledge."[1]

Measure here does not mean something quantitative. It has nothing to do with "measuring"in the ordinary sense of the word, nor with the ethical concept of "proper measure." "Measure" as an ontological concept means something qualitative, something belonging to the realm of form and substance. Moreover, the concept of measure includes a kind of causality.[2] This meaning can still be seen in our concept of the "standard."

The concept of measure is represented and actualized in three realms of reality, or rather three relations of reality: the relation of God and creature, the relation of the artist to his work and the relation between the objective world of being and human knowledge.

The inherent nature of something real is that which causes it to be what it is. But every created reality is not only what it is through its inherent nature. Every created reality is related to a creator who brought it into existence and formed it, and through whom it is what it is. To speak more exactly, every created reality is what it is—apart from its inherent nature and anterior to it—through its relation to a creative knowledge, a creative intelligence.[3] Through the creative will a reality possesses its existence, the fact *that* it is; through the creative knowledge a reality possesses its quality, *what* it is.[4] (The concepts "what," "nature," "true," pertain to knowledge; the concepts "that," "existence," "good," pertain to the will.) The creative intellect, of God or of the human artist, forms within itself a pattern of the reality to be created; it "pre-forms" within itself the form or nature of the reality. And because of this pre-forming, creative knowledge, the intellect, or rather the pattern which has been formed in it, becomes the "measure" of the reality.

The concept of measure must be understood through the concept of form or nature. The measure of a reality is its "external" form. It is, as Master Eckhart said, the "preceding image." The measure is, in a very precise sense, the "model" of the reality. The inherent form of a reality is, as scholastic philosophy expresses it, its "interior formal cause." The measure of a reality is its "exterior formal cause," through which, as well as through the interior formal cause and anterior to this, it is what it is.

The statement of St. Thomas, "*Deus omnium entium est mensura*," that is, God is the measure of all things,[5] means simply this: through the creative knowledge of God all real things are what they are; the divine knowledge is their exterior formal cause; all created things have their pre-form, their model, in the intellect of God; the interior forms of all reality exist as "ideas," as "preceding images" in God.

And similarly the statement that the artist is the measure of his work[6] means: the work is pre-formed in the creative knowledge of the artist; in this there exists the model of the work. The idea that has taken form in the creative knowledge of the artist is the "exterior" form of the work, through which it is what it is.

The relation of the "exterior formal cause" exists also between objective being and the intellect of man, whose cognition—as a perception of reality—is not creative but receptive. The realization of the intellect in the act, the "that" of cognition, proceeds from the spontaneous power of the subject; and this spontaneity of the mind, which in the order of being surpasses every non-rational creature, must not be "objectivistically" underrated. But the "what" of cognition stems only from the object. The object, the reality, the thing, these are the "exterior" form of the intellect, through which it is "what" it is.

"Created things, from which our intellect receives knowledge, give the measure to our intellect. But they have received their measure from the divine intellect, in which all created things are as all objects of art are in the mind of the artist. Thus, the divine intellect gives the measure and does not receive the measure. But created things both give and receive the measure. But our intellect, in regard to natural objects, is receptive of the measure and does not give the measure. It does this only in regard to artefacts."[7]

The statement that objective reality is the measure of our knowledge means precisely this: The real objects are the pre-forms and models of that which our mind cognitively forms and actually is. The world of knowledge is "pre-formed" in the objective world of being; the latter is the original image, the former the copy. The intellect "in act" is of its nature an imitation; it has an essential relation to something anterior in its nature. This something which naturally precedes all cognition is reality. The intellect is not "of itself"; it is something secondary and essentially dependent. "The intellect receives its measure from objects; that is, human knowledge is true not of itself, but it is true because and insofar as it conforms to reality."[8]

At first sight it seems rather unfitting that objects should be the models determining the "what" of our knowledge as the creative knowledge of God bestows the "what" upon objects. We may remark that such analogies and examples are not intended or able to bridge the abyss of the *analogia entis*, which, moreover, like the sea, is both abyss and bridge. St. Thomas, again, who thought and wrote most profoundly about the transcendence of God over all created power, does not hesitate to say: "God is the measure of all that is; he is, therefore, related to all other beings as the objects of knowledge are related to our knowledge and constitute its measure."[9]

But that which provides the measure, the *mensura*, and that which receives the measure, the *mensuratum*, are identical in their "what."

The interior essential form of the creature, insofar as it is really itself, is in its "what" no different from the "exterior" idea of the creative intelligence of God. The work of art, insofar as it has really "emerged" into visible reality, is essentially identical with its original model in the mind of the artist, and the "what" of our knowledge, insofar as it is true, is identical with the original "what" of real objects, which are the measure of knowledge. But we certainly must not overlook the qualifying statement "insofar as it is true."

Mensura and *mensuratum*, that which provides the measure and that which receives the measure, differ only in their different positions in the order of importance and meaning involved in their realization. That which provides the measure is, in its quality of model and original form, identical with the recipient of the measure. That which receives the measure is, in its quality of image and copy, the very measure itself.

Our knowledge, then, as image and copy, is reality itself.

The Identity of Mind and Reality

The same thing is expressed by another fundamental principle of the realist epistemology; it differs from the first one, which is more dynamic, in having a more static character. This second fundamental principle is expressed as follows: In knowledge the intellect and the known reality become one[1]; "the intellect is wholly—that is, in a perfect manner, the known object"[2]; "the soul becomes, so to speak, transformed into the real object"[3]; the act of knowledge brings about identity between the mind and reality.[4]

The statements we have quoted, all of which are taken from the work of St. Thomas Aquinas, have become so strange to us that we consider it quite self-evident that they are meant to be taken only in a "figurative" way. Even many a "Thomist" takes refuge in vague limitations and restrictions, maintaining that of course there is no question of a "real" and "actual" identity here. The "naive" epistemology of the Middle Ages seems to us moderns, if not absurd, at least excessively and unduly simplified, and we indulge in the consideration that between St. Thomas and ourselves there intervenes the *Critique of Pure Reason*. But we must not forget that even the mature Goethe, who like ourselves belongs to the post-Kantian age, said that what we express about objects constitutes "the real objects in our conception"[5]; and a few years before his death (1829) he wrote in his *Maxims and Reflections:* "There is a delicate empiricism which identifies itself intimately with the object, and thereby becomes an actual experience."[6]

The identity between the intellect and the object,

a true and actual self-sameness, is brought about by the immaterial, spiritual image of reality which impresses itself upon the intellect, as the seal impresses itself upon the wax. "The intellect is the known reality through the intelligible image of the reality."[7] In the image, the super-material core of "what-ness" of the real, formed by the creative intellect and adapted to cognition on the part of the created intellect, presents itself. It is the proper task of the spontaneous power of our mind (called *intellectus agens* by St. Thomas[8]), which shares in and resembles the original divine spontaneity, to free this super-material core of "what-ness" in the real object from its material limitations. And in this illumination of sense-data by the *intellectus agens* the essentially spiritual cognition, accessible only to the immaterial "what-ness," is prepared and made possible, as the reality is raised to the state of immediate knowability.

The intelligible image, then, is on the one hand a representation of reality; indeed, in the "what" it is identical with the objective reality. "The intelligible image is in a certain sense the essence and nature of the reality itself, not according to natural being, but according to intelligible being."[9] But "natural being" and "intelligible being" are two ways of being, so to speak, of the same reality. They are related to each other as are the concepts "true" and "being"; and truth, if the term is used not of the judgment but of the reality itself, means nothing else than the quality of being knowable.[10] The "intelligible" being of an object is the "natural" being of the same thing, insofar as this thing is true, that is, knowable. Truth and being are really identical; "the true in objects is essentially the same as being."[11]

The reason why all these statements approach the borders of the tautological is that we are here dealing with matters that are primary and self-evident in the most literal sense, and which in every effort to explain them become repetitious and trite. "The intelligible image, then, through which the reality is known, is necessarily the essence of the reality itself."[12]

On the other hand the intelligible image which is impressed upon the intellect becomes the interior essential form of the cognitive power, which is raised to "act" through this formation, that is, which realizes its potentiality. Before the intellect is "in act" it is, as Aristotle says in his book on the soul,[13] "nothing in regard to reality." And St. Thomas says, "The potential capacity of our intellect has the same place in the order of cognition that prime matter has in the order of natural objects."[14] This means that our intellect, like prime matter at the beginning of creation, is a substantial potentiality of being, a pure possibility, receptive of being, not yet qualitatively or quantitatively determined, but awaiting determination and formation, until it rises to the point of self-realization by means of the intellectual images of the real.

Before this transformation, and only then, is the intellect in a condition of non-identity with reality.

In the measure of its self-realization it also realizes its identity with the objective world of being.[15]

The statement that the intellectual image is the interior essential form of the intellect "in act" can be completely understood only if we remember that "interior essential form" means simply that by which something is what it is. "As the soul is not something different from the man," so the intellectual image is "not something different from the intellect, but the same thing."[16] The intellectual image and the intellect are identical; it is the identity of the interior essential form of a reality with this reality itself. Indeed, the intellect and the transforming and realizing intellectual image of a reality are in a higher sense and to a greater degree identical than the potentiality of knowing before cognition and "in the act" of cognition is identical with itself. "The concept has a closer relationship to the reality conceived than it has to the one conceiving it, although the concept dwells in the one conceiving it, who is its bearer."[17] "Through the intellectual image, which is the interior essential form of the intellect, the intellect is the reality itself."[18]

The Superior General of the Dominicans, Franciscus Sylvestris (Ferrariensis), in his famous commentary on the *Summa contra Gentiles*, carried on this idea as follows: "The nature and perfection of being of the reality which exists in the objective world of being are taken up into the intellect; they bring it to the perfection of being. But because every being is what it is by virtue of its interior form, it follows that the intelligence in act is the known reality itself. For it knows in act because and insofar as the interior form of the known reality is within it. He who knows a stone is a stone, for all that possesses the interior form of a stone is a stone. However, we cannot say that the intellect which knows a stone is simply and absolutely a stone, for the essential form of the stone exists in the intellect in an intelligible way and not in its natural existence. Hence, the intellect which knows a stone is a stone in an intelligible way. The intelligence, then, which is transformed by the intelligible image of a reality can be called the reality itself because it possesses the form by which the reality is what it is."[19] The "what" of our intellect in act is identical with the "what" of the reality upon which it is fixed in knowing. At the same time this reality of course remains in its concrete and natural "that," in its existence, really separate and different from the concrete and natural "that" of the act of knowing and of the knower himself. The known reality in our intellect ("as" something known) and the real object existing in objective reality are identical in their essence; they are different in the manner of being of this "what," in their existence.

The nature of knowledge lies in this relationship of essential identity and existential difference.

The attempt to clarify completely this relation of the two equally real situations, the attainment of reality and the separateness of consciousness, necessarily leads us to the limits of knowledge. A recognition of the mysterious character of knowledge is "the true result of a critique of knowledge."[20]

Knowledge and Truth

The relation of the mind and objective reality to each other has three names; regarded from the point of view of the mind it is called "cognition," regarded from the point of view of reality it is called "being known," regarded from the point of view of both together it is called "truth."

"Intelligent beings are distinguished from non-intelligent beings in this way, that the non-intelligent have no form but their own; but the intelligent being is capable of having also the form of another being.—That is why the philosopher says that the soul is in a certain manner all things."[1]

To *have* a form means to be something definite. Everything is what it is through the form which it has.

To know, then, means to have the forms of other things, to be the other, to be identical with the other, to be all things. "That is why the philosopher says that the soul *is* all things." To know is to become another.[2]

We must distinguish between the process of cognition and knowledge as an accomplished fact. The process of cognition is both active and passive. Actively it is the separation of the super-material, intelligible core of being of the objects from the sensible shell of matter; a spontaneous penetration into the realm of immaterial essentiality through which the intellect really comes to the active realization of its own self. Passively it consists of the admission, the reception, of the essential form of the reality.

This active-passive process is unessential in regard to knowledge as an accomplished fact; or rather, this activity and passivity is necessary for knowledge to come about but it does not constitute the essence of actual knowledge.[3] The essence of knowledge is the *possession* of the forms of objective reality; knowledge as an accomplished fact is not an "activity" of the intellect but its realization. It is the relation of the mind to objective reality. It is the identity between the knowing soul and the reality, regarded from the point of view of the knowing soul, which in this identity realizes its own potentiality.[4]

It is this very relation of the intellect and the reality which constitutes the conceptual content of "truth." Truth is the conformity *(conformitas)* and the assimilation *(adaequatio)*—taking both terms in their most exact sense—of reality and knowledge. And this relation is realized in the very act of knowledge: "In the operation of the intellect there is accomplished the relation of assimilation in which lies the essence of truth."[5] Truth is nothing else than the relation of identity between the mind and the reality, a relation consisting in and accomplished in knowledge, and in this relation the reality is the measure of the intellect.

Objectivity as an Attitude in Knowing

The nature of knowledge rests upon objectivity as the only proper attitude of man. (Objectivity as an ethical attitude in a narrower sense shall be discussed in the second section.) If we demand objectivity in knowing, this means simply that knowledge must be really knowledge. Nothing else is involved here but the true character of knowledge.

Knowledge is the relation between the subject and the object, determined in its "that" by the subject, in its "what" by the object. So the activity and the influence of the subject upon knowledge is—insofar as real, that is, true, knowledge is concerned—confined to the positing of its existence. The content, the "what," the nature of the knowledge, is determined solely by the matter, the thing, the object—insofar as we are dealing with true knowledge. If then any determination of the content by the will of the subject enters into the knowledge, if the subject wishes one thing to be so, something to be different and something else not to be at all, then, as far as this personal subjective influence extends, there is actually no knowledge at all.

This does not mean that ultimate passivity is the proper attitude in regard to knowledge or the suitable attitude for man in general. First of all, a tremendous activity of the will is required if we are to be determined only by reality in our knowing, to be objective and to force ourselves to silence and keep ourselves out of the picture, and so to become perceptive. We are beginning to understand once more the meaning of objectivity in perception, to recognize that there can and must be a kind of asceticism of knowledge.

Secondly, the spontaneously moving penetration by the mind of the intellectually knowable nature of reality, which prepares for the actual knowing, is really a supreme activity. Of this we have already spoken.

Moreover, thirdly, there is a place for the individual view of the subject, which differs in regard to the content of knowledge, if only because of the variety of the objective reality, which appears to different persons in different ways, but to each one as it really is.

Finally, the will of the subject and his affirmative or negative or indifferent attitude toward the object will, of course, definitely determine the intensity and the direction of his attention and awareness. But this influence of the subject does not affect the "what" of knowledge, but only its "that," the setting up and carrying out of the "objective" of knowledge.[1]

Another argument basic for objectivity lies in the order of the objects of knowledge, which is in a certain sense a hierarchy. Here we can deal with this only summarily.

The human intellect first knows the objective being presented to it, thereafter the act of knowing, the faculty of knowing and the knowing subject itself as subject.[2]

That—and in what sense—this order, in which the object precedes the subject, is also a hierarchy may be seen in the following statements of St. Thomas: "Nobody knows that he knows except by the fact that he knows something; for knowing something precedes one's knowing oneself as knowing." "Our intellect cannot know itself by being immediately aware of itself; but by being aware of something else it comes to know itself."[3]

That means, the intellect itself becomes knowable only when it has taken into itself the essential form of an objective reality, for it is only in this way that it attains true self-realization, and a thing is knowable only in the measure in which it is real. Only through the entrance of objective reality into our being do we reach our true selfhood. Only on the basis of and by means of knowledge of the objective world of being does the intellect enter the realm of that which can be its own object. Goethe says: "A man knows himself only insofar as he knows the world."

Section II

The Unity of Theoretical and Practical Reason

Human reason by realizing itself through knowledge, refers back to the objective world of being upon which it is dependent, by which it is interiorly formed, and with which it is identical. To this basic statement of realist epistemology Christian occidental philosophy adds as "intellectualistic" ethics, the statement: the free moral action of man refers back to the reason, upon which it is dependent and by which it is interiorly formed.

To clarify the relation between these two theses we must first make some distinctions.

First of all, we must not overlook the fact that in these statements the word "reason" has two meanings. In the first statement it means the theoretical, speculative reason, in the second the practical reason. Reason is "theoretical" when it is turned receptively toward the real objects presented to it. Reason is practical when it turns toward acting *(agere)* and making *(facere)*.

Thus, the chain by which the good is bound to reality is composed of the following links: objective reality, theoretical reason, practical reason, moral action. After showing that, and how, the first two links are connected, and before speaking of the connection of the last two, we must grasp the relation of the theoretical and the practical reason.

Theoretical reason itself becomes "in extending," *per extensionem*, the practical reason.[1] "The practical reason, like the speculative, knows the truth, but it orders the known truth toward action"[2]; through the extension of knowledge toward willing and acting, the theoretical reason becomes practical.

This means first of all that the theoretical and the practical reason are not two distinct powers of the soul.[3] Nor are they two separate and independent operations of one and the same "basic faculty."

This is how Kant seems to understand the relation of the theoretical and the practical reason. He speaks of a "common principle" of both[4] and of the "speculative use of reason" and of the "practical use of reason."[5] In spite of their being rooted in a single theoretical-practical "basic faculty," Kant makes the practical reason entirely independent of the theoretical and of all that can be the object of theoretical activity, that means, independent of all knowledge of reality.

Moreover, this is not a harmless unessential speculation for philosophers. In making the practical reason—that is, the power of the soul that determines action—independent of the theoretical reason—that is, the power of the soul that perceives objective being—Kant sees, according to Richard Kroner, nothing less than "the conquest of the metaphysics of being, the transfer of the center of gravity from the object to the subject."[6] Therefore, our examination of reality and the good might be quite correct in considering the unity of the theoretical and the practical reason, and the priority of the theoretical reason upon which this unity is based, to be precisely the ontological foundation of ethics and the starting point for a transfer of the center of gravity from the subject back to the object, to objective reality.

The concept of the practical reason necessarily includes and asserts the theoretical reason as well. The "basic faculty" is the theoretical reason, which "extends" to become the practical. The theoretical includes the practical, somewhat as the genus includes the distinct species. Only insofar as it is theoretical is the reason also practical. Prior to all action is the "theoretic" perception of reality. *Intellectus speculativus fit practicus*, the theoretic reason "becomes" practical.[7] All that is practical is rooted in the theoretical and presupposes it.

If we consider the relationship of the *object* of the theoretical reason to that of the practical reason, the result is the same. The proper object of the theoretical reason is the truth in things. The proper object of the practical reason is "the true as the measure of action,"[8] "the true which extends into the good."[9] The object of the theoretical reason includes and comprises the object of the practical reason. The object of the theoretical reason, the true, "becomes" the object of the practical reason by establishing a relation with the object of the will.

The practical reason, then, is nothing but the theoretical reason itself regarded under the aspect of a special function. But we must note this: It is not quite correct to say that classical-Christian philosophy maintains an actual "primacy" of the theoretical reason over the practical reason and of theory over practice in general. "Primacy" in the strict sense can exist only in the relationship of realities which are independent of each other. There can be "primacy" in the relation of St. Peter to the other apostles, and Kant can also speak of a real primacy in the relation of the practical reason to the theoretical. But it is not possible to speak of a primacy of the foundation over the building, for the building includes the foundation. And this same relation exists between the theoretical and the practical reason.

The "extension" by which the theoretical reason becomes practical, is directed, as we said, toward willing and action. This "particular function" of direction toward the will consists in the deciding, commanding, guiding causation of free action. We shall speak of this in detail.

But we can already see the outline of the situation. Reason, as practical reason, would not be turned toward willing and action if it had not previously, as theoretical reason, also been turned toward things. It could not be decisive and commanding if it were not first made accessible to being through knowledge. It would not be the measure of action if it did not first receive its measure from objective reality.

The decision to do a definite thing, which is an interior "command" *(imperium)* given to ourselves by ourselves, and which precedes a free action, does not come blindly and at random. Knowledge of being is "lengthened" and transformed into decision and command. The imperative is founded upon an indicative; the latter makes the former possible. Essentially prior to the decision and command is the purely perceptive statement. The "image" of the real precedes and underlies the "plan" of all realization.

Decision and command, in which the practical reason is realized, signify, then, a knowledge which turns toward the will. But knowledge is an essential identity of the mind with the objective reality.

The relation of these two facts reveals the measure and the manner in which the practical reason proper, which on its part determines the free act, is essentially bound up with the objective reality which is perceived in our knowledge of being. This also gives us a clear view of the purpose of our task: to show in detail how, in the fact that action is determined by knowledge, action is really determined by the objective reality itself.

The Structure of Moral Action

The extension of the reason, which perceives reality, toward willing and action is not begun and ended in a single act. But this turning toward the will gradually increases in intensity, moving step by step through the numerous partial acts of which moral action as a whole is composed, and so becomes the decision and command directed immediately toward action.

The partial acts of which, as we said, moral action is composed, are acts of knowledge and of will, and those of the will are so arranged that every single act of knowledge is followed by an act of will. "Because the will follows the reason, the process of the will corresponds to that of the reason."[1] In the gradation of the cognitive partial acts the self-extension of the reason toward the will is realized; in the succession of these cognitive partial acts the reason becomes practical.

It is not that in the continued succession of acts the theoretical disappears, so to speak, for it is the theoretical reason itself which becomes practical through its extension toward the will; it is the cognitive reason turned toward reality, which, as practical, gives its commands to the will.

It is indispensable at this point to give a brief, perhaps too condensed, but necessarily somewhat "academic" account of the structure of moral action.[5] (The diagram on page 120 may serve to make the account more clear.)

The first prerequisite for effective willing is the knowledge of the end, or, what amounts to the same thing, the good[3] that shall be attained or realized. "The awareness of the end must be considered the first thing in the realm of action."[4] Only through knowledge does that which is to be realized come within the range and reach of the man who acts. "The good, under the aspect of the true, has a relation to the reason that is prior to that which, under the aspect of something to be striven for, it has to the will; for the will could not turn toward the good if this had not first been grasped by the reason."[5] Seeing the good is the first and lowest level of cognitive acts in the structure of moral action.

This is followed by the first volitional act of simple "willing" *(volitio)*, the love of the good as such. "In the volitional sphere love is the prime source of any movement toward an end."[6]

The first cognitive act, the sight of the good, is purely perceptive, theoretical, "speculative," mirroring the reality. Hence, the order in which "simple willing follows" the sight of the good is not based upon a causality of the reason formally directed toward the will and in any way "imperative." The cause of the order is that the reason "presents" its object to the will.

The reason becomes practical in the proper sense, that is, deciding, commanding and directing, only at the second stage of the cognitive partial act, in the imperative voice of the primordial conscience *(synderesis)*.[7] In this act of the primordial conscience the reason begins to be practical; here the extension to the will begins. In the voice of the primordial conscience moral action as such also commences. The practical insight of the primordial conscience corresponds to the theoretical insight into the supreme basic principles of thought. The primordial conscience is the supreme awareness – transcending and independent of all efforts of thought – of the primary, basic first principles of action,[8] summed up in the imperative: We must love the good.[9]

In the order of the acts of the will, the imperative voice of the primordial conscience is followed by the "striving" for the end *(intentio finis).* It is distinguished from the first act of the will – the simple willing – in the same way as the act of the primordial conscience is distinguished from the mere sight of the good. The theoretic intelligence first sees the good as such; the primordial conscience, in its practical knowledge, considers the good as the motive and source of action. Thus, the "willing" is directed to the good as such, the "striving" considers the good as the goal of the free movement of the willing person, that is, the end of its action.[10]

The next action of the practical reason is "the consideration of what is to be done," the *consilium*, taking counsel with oneself.[11] The command of the primordial conscience and the "striving" are directed toward the end; the consideration and the following partial acts have to do with the means to the end.[12]

The consideration may lead to the conclusion that there are several appropriate means to accomplish the end. To this "intermediate" conclusion of the consideration there corresponds, on the part of the acts of will, the "consent" *(consensus)* of the will to the entirety of the appropriate means.[13]

The real final conclusion of the consideration is the "judgment"[14] that among the totality of the appropriate means *one* definite way to the end is recognized as the one to be taken rather than the others.

To this judgment the will responds by the "decision" *(electio)*.[15] This choice of the will is the actual definite willing, the decision for something concrete and therewith the exclusion of all other possibilities.[16]

If the consideration throughout reveals only one means to realize the end, then the "consent" and the "choice" coincide.[17]

The final cognitive partial act, in which the extension of the reason toward action is completed, is the "resolution" or "command" *(imperium)*, the immediate order given to the will to "use" the chosen means.[18] In this command the reason becomes in the final and pre-eminent sense "practical reason." "To command is the proper function of the practical reason."[19]

The will obeys the command of the reason in arousing the powers of the person and "using" them *(usus activus)* to carry out the command. This execution is nothing but the "use" *(usus passivus)* of human powers by the will.[20]

It is probably not necessary to protect this enumeration of the steps of moral action against the naive misunderstanding that it means something more than a diagrammatic summary. This claims, however, to follow faithfully, though with some simplification, the structure of the moral activity of the will.

The actual principle of the succession of the theoretic partial acts, from the first sight of the good to the immediate concrete command given to the will, is the extension of the reason toward will and action which is realized in this process. The dependence of the will upon knowledge increases, in the succession of the partial acts, from a purely factual "following" to a real "obedience" to the reason, which in the act of "commanding" avails itself of this dependence. The causality of the reason, as directed toward the will, buds in the simple sight of the good. It works more plainly in the voice of the primordial conscience, which is a formal command, even though not very concrete. It unfolds fully and finally when the practical reason takes the will into its service in the act of the concrete "command," which immediately precedes the properly executive action of the will.[21]

Another mark, also basic to the nature of this succession of partial acts of reason, is this: every succeeding act is more concrete and less general than the preceding one. The voice of the primordial conscience is directed very generally toward *the* good as the end of human action; in the "choice" the reason chooses *one* particular way to the end, whereas the "consideration" which precedes the judgment is concerned with a number of ways.

This mark of increasing particularization reflects the first sign of the increasing extension of the reason toward the will. Reason as such grasps what is general, but the will strives toward particular objects.[22]

We shall name a final mark of this succession of acts: each succeeding act has less of necessity and certainty than the preceding one. The primordial conscience is unerring.[23] Its voice "is always right"[24] and "never makes a mistake."[25] "Just as in the theoretical sphere the reason cannot err about the first basic principles, so it cannot be mistaken about the first basic principles of action. Therefore, we say that the primordial conscience is indestructible."[26] But consideration, choice and command are by no means free from the possibility of error.

Now we must explain how in the individual partial acts the fact that the practical reason is determined by reality is connected with its function of originating and determining action.

This explanation will be divided into two sections. The first deals with the primordial conscience, its relation to objective reality and its relation to will and action.

The second section sums up the remaining partial acts of the practical reason—consideration, choice, and command—under the aspect of prudence. For the virtue of prudence is nothing else than the art of considering, deciding and commanding rightly.[27] Here too we shall see the determining nature of reality on the one hand and the relation to action on the other.

The Voice of the Primordial Conscience

The primordial conscience is a natural, innate "attitude" *(habitus)* of the human mind by which it is destined to have a primary and infallible judgment about the good as the end and the meaning of human action. The voice of the primordial conscience is—as to its content—the natural moral law. The primordial conscience is the natural awareness of the ethical natural law.[1]

The voice of the primordial conscience is the practical basic principle, simply and absolutely, upon which the whole moral motivation of rational beings depends. "The original direction of all our actions toward the end is necessarily brought about by the natural law."[2]

The practical basic principle governs the whole sphere of the practical just as the theoretic basic principle, the law of identity, governs the whole sphere of theoretical thinking. The law of identity is based upon the concept of being; the voice of the primordial conscience is based upon the concept of the good.[3]

There are two modes of a rational judgment (and the primordial conscience definitely belongs to the sphere of reason[4]): the mode of the pure statement, the indicative *(modus enuntiandi)* and the mode of command, the imperative *(modus praecipiendi)*.[5]

The fact of being based upon the concept of the good is by itself not the supreme basic principle of the practical reason; for the definition of the good, which is a purely indicative statement ("The good is that toward which everything strives"[6]), is also based upon the *concept* of the good. But it is immediately evident that the basic principle of the practical reason must be stated differently. The practical is a movement of being, governed by the mind. Hence, the basic principle of the practical must contain within itself this movement, still potential, as its cause, source and essence. But the definition of the good, although based upon the concept of the good, is purely theoretic and static. It does not have the dynamic element, the element of motion. This dynamic element is found in the other mode of the reasoned judgment, in the imperative. The structure of the imperative is: this must be that. The "must be" is the expression and the medium of motion. Therefore, in order that the indicative definition of the good may "extend" to become the practical basic principle, this "must be" must enter into it. The good must be that toward which everything strives. In other words: we must love the good, *bonum faciendum est.*[7]

Now we can formulate the practical basic principle, the voice of the primordial conscience: "The supreme principle of the practical reason is based upon the concept of the good, which is as follows: the good is that toward which everything strives. So this is the supreme statement of the law: We must do and love the good, and we must avoid the evil."[8]

The dynamic, imperative character of the primordial conscience is derived from a preliminary act of the will. All movement comes from the will.

"Reason also receives its motive power from the will."[9] This act of the will which precedes the voice of the primordial conscience is the simple willing of the natural love for the good. "The order of the natural law follows the order of the natural inclinations of our being."[10] Of this we shall speak in greater detail.

The relation of the primordial conscience and its voice to the concrete moral action is brought about by the "striving" and the other partial acts, which in the diagrammatic sketch of the total moral action lie between the voice of the primordial conscience and the "carrying out" of the concrete command of the practical reason.

The relation of command and obedience is found directly in the dependence of the "striving" upon the voice of the primordial conscience. The "striving" is the answer and the immediate obedience of the will to the ethical natural law formulated in the voice of the primordial conscience: "The good must be the end of human action." The "striving" is the reply: "I *will* the good as the end of my action."[11]

The rightness of this act of the will is the foundation of prudence[12] and so of the rightness of all the succeeding partial acts of the practical reason.[13] The "consideration"[14] and the "command"[15] are rooted in this act of striving for the end. It is time to call to the reader's attention that the determination of willing and action by the voice of the primordial conscience is already beginning to appear in outline.

The wholly concrete moral action of the will is

entirely and immediately formed by and dependent upon the concrete "command" of the practical reason. But the concrete command of the practical reason is in a very definite way related to the earlier general voice of the primordial conscience. And this relation determines the dependence of the concrete moral action upon the primordial conscience itself.

In the voice of the primordial conscience ("the good must be loved"), the material and formal basic structure of all concrete "commands" of the practical reason is given, just as the material and formal basic structure of all concrete individual statements is found in the principle of identity ("that which is, is").

This statement, which expresses the dependence of the concrete "command" upon the voice of the primordial conscience, requires a brief explanation. In every judgment we distinguish between "matter" and "form." The subject and the predicate are the logical "matter"; the copula is the logical "form." In combining or dividing the subject and the predicate, it expresses a judgment about what it is. In every individual theoretical judgment—whose pattern is "this is that," the matter ("this," "that") and the form ("is")—the structure of the principle of identity recurs; the final statement that can be made about every "this" and "that" is that it "is." The principle of identity states that whatever is, is. The concrete, theoretical individual judgment states that *this* which is, is. Hence, the principle of identity, material and formal, is the basic structure of every concrete statement.

In the same way the voice of the primordial conscience, which is the "principle of identity" in the realm of the practical, affects all the concrete imperatives of the practical reason. The voice of the primordial conscience says: "The good, whatever it may be, must be." Every concrete "command" of the practical reason says: "*This* good must be." So the "principle of identity" of the primordial conscience is likewise the basic structure materially and formally affecting and regulating all the commands of the practical reason.

The other question, whether the primordial conscience is determined by objective reality, cannot be answered, anymore than the first question, by the means provided by empirical psychology. The voice of the primordial conscience is a purely natural thing, preceding all possibility of conscious control. But the question is not really put in this way. It means this: Does the voice of the primordial conscience necessarily presuppose a definite relation to objective reality?

To this we must reply, first of all, that certainly the voice of the primordial conscience presupposes a knowledge and awareness of reality.[16] The imperative of the primordial conscience would not be possible without a preceding knowledge. It is, like every command of the practical reason, a transformed knowledge. "To command means to apply knowledge to willing and action."[17]

The imperative *form* of that voice is derived, as we have said, from a preceding act of the will. But the *content*, that which is commanded, the *matter*, comes from the theoretic reason, which is turned toward reality. The "what" of the imperative of the primordial conscience is based upon knowledge, its "that" is based upon the will. If the will were not active, no imperative could come about; the "must be" would be unthinkable. But the "must be" would be without content if, before the imperative, the intelligence had not been aware of being.

Knowledge is relation to objective reality, identity of the mind with the world of being. So it is the same thing if we say that the voice of the primordial conscience includes knowledge or if we say that it presupposes a relation to reality.

The knowledge which is included in and presupposed by the voice of the primordial conscience is the knowledge of the good. "It is peculiar to the primordial conscience to oppose the evil and to strive for the good; but it could not do this if it had not first really known the good and the evil."[18] The content and basis of the primordial conscience is the concept of the good, *fundatur supra rationem boni.* The knowledge of the nature of the good becomes imperative in the voice of the primordial conscience.

But knowledge of the nature of the good necessarily includes the previous awareness of the essential structure of reality as such.[20]

"The good is that for which all things strive." But what is it that all beings strive for? "All beings strive for their perfection."[21] "The good" is perfection and all that conduces to it.[22]

The concept of perfection, which here, in a sense

transcending the ethical, is taken to mean fullness of being (having become filled or complete), includes and comprises these concepts: imperfection, the perfecting process, possibility of being (potency), realization, reality (act), becoming. Therefore, as St. Thomas expressly states, the word *perfectio*, in the strict sense, cannot be applied to God.[23]

In every reality there is "that" and "what," existence and essence. In God existence and essence are absolutely identical. In a finite creature, however, essence and existence are distinct. The creature "is" its nature only in germ *(in potentia)*. It "becomes" the nature which is to be realized. God alone is absolutely "in being"; the creature, man, is "becoming." "Becoming" is the transition of essence from the state of germinal potency to the state of actuality. At the beginning of every becoming there is a minimally realized essence, at its end (perhaps unattainable) there is a maximal, realized, completely perfected essence. The "formula" of this movement is: the real becomes what it is.

But the good is nothing else than this goal and end of the movement of being, the realization of the essence. "Everything has as much of goodness as it has of being."[24] Perfection and the good mean nothing else than the "plenitude of being," *plenitudo essendi*.[25] The source which feeds the movement of anything real is the natural inclination of every being to become what it is.[26] And because the good, in this sense, has the character of a goal and end, "it happens that the reason naturally seizes as a good everything toward which man has a natural inclination."[27] The good, then, is that toward which the real naturally moves; but this is its own realization. The good is the real fulfilled in being; the good is the real at the goal of its movement.

Hence, the voice of the primordial conscience says: the real should move toward that toward which it tends by its nature to move.[28] This expresses, first of all, a total affirmation of the meaning of the world. Secondly, the voice of the primordial conscience, as the basic first principle of human action, indicates the ethical necessity of man's conscious self-coordination with the direction of the movement of total reality.

This meaning of the primordial conscience and its voice become clearer if we consider the natural law, which, as we have already said, is immediately related to the primordial conscience.

"The natural law is nothing else than the participation of the rational creature in the eternal law."[29]

"The eternal law is the voice of divine wisdom which moves all things toward the proper end."[30] St. Thomas understands the concept of law somewhat differently than our present usage. We think of "law" as the objective command, which, after it has been expressed, has a kind of independent existence between the lawgiver and the people. St. Thomas sees in the law above all the *act* of commanding, as it is really existent in the mind of the lawgiver: *in principe existens.*[31] The eternal law, as the divine command addressed to the whole of reality, is so effective that every natural inclination in creatures is nothing else than its expression bearing witness to and affirming itself. This divine command is so intrinsic to reality that it is actually identical with the interior operation of the nature of things. If we take the eternal law, in the sense in which the concept of law is at present generally understood, as the objective command of the lawgiver, which has, so to speak, taken up its own position, then we can define it as the inherent directive of total reality itself, which has received and continues to receive its impulse from the wisdom of God.

And the natural law "not different from the eternal law"[32] is nothing else than this very inherent directive of all reality insofar as it is recognized and affirmed by man who, through his reason, participates in the eternal law. The natural law demands of rational creatures first of all the affirmation, the imitative carrying out, and the preservation of the natural order of the world.[33] Secondly and essentially, it demands that man must place himself under the obligation of the sentence, "Become what you are," a statement in which the inherent direction of all reality is expressed. It is reason, the basis and the means of that "participation in the eternal law,"[34] which reveals to man his own inherent direction toward self-realization. Through his rational knowledge man can take the law of his being which inheres in him and make it his own commanding voice, whereas irrational creatures follow the law of their being only passively. It is not present within them as their own act. Upon this recognition of the natural inclination of being all virtue depends. "The virtues make us able to follow in the proper manner our natural inclinations which belong to the natural law."[35]

Much more could be said about the concepts of the eternal and the natural law, on which the whole ethics of St. Thomas and of classical theology is built. But even these brief remarks have probably revealed something of the secret bond connecting the primordial conscience with objective reality.

The voice of the primordial conscience, which is the basic principle of all human action, is determined by being, which presents itself to cognition. The determination is as follows: The knowledge—connected with reality—of the basic structure of all beings and, above all, of man himself, in other words, the knowledge of the urge toward self-realization, born of the tension between existence and essence, which are not identical, is transformed into the command of the primordial conscience. The natural basic structure of reality, above all of man himself, is, in the voice of the primordial conscience, turned to the will. It is knowledge become command, and it carries with it an obligation. The fundamental essential structural "law" of reality, by means of natural knowledge, becomes, in the voice of the primordial conscience, the basic *moral* law of all human action.

Prudence[1]

The voice of the primordial conscience is always "right." Consideration, judgment and command can be right or wrong, true or false.[2] The right consideration, the right judgment and—above all—the right concrete command, these are the acts of the virtue of prudence. The primordial conscience is the naturally and necessarily correct disposition of the practical reason, insofar as it passes judgment about the end and goal of human action. Prudence is the proper disposition of the practical reason insofar as it knows what is to be done concretely in the matter of ways and means. Prudence is not guaranteed by natural necessity as the primordial conscience is; it is the fruit of fallible knowledge and of the free decision of the will.

Prudence is, as St. Thomas says, partly cognitive (*cognoscitiva*) and partly commanding (*praeceptiva*).[3] The commanding quality of prudence, into which "consideration" and "judgment" flow, is the expression of its relation to concrete willing and acting; the cognitive quality is the expression of its determination by the objective world of being.

The dependence of willing and acting upon prudence lies in this: the command of prudence is the "measure" of the concrete moral action of the will.[4]

It may at first seem surprising that here the same concept of measure appears which we found in the relation of reality to our knowledge. At least one might have some doubt whether "measure" here meant exactly the same as it does there. But at any rate St. Thomas undeniably understood the term "measure" in the same sense in regard to the dependence of willing and working upon the command of prudence and in regard to the formation of knowledge by reality. He expressly compares, under the aspect of "measure," the relation of reality and knowledge and the relation of the practical reason to concrete moral action.[5] Both relations are symbolized by the image of the relation of the artist and his work.[6] Furthermore, the causality of the measure is presented to us as the "exterior formal cause," and St. Thomas attributes this same formal causality to the command of prudence in its relation to the whole sphere of moral actions and virtues.[7] Finally, to describe the relation of prudence to moral action, St. Thomas uses the words "identity" and "conformity," which are also used to describe the relation of knowledge to reality.[8]

In the command of prudence the morally good action is "pre-formed." Through it the action is "what" it is. The command of prudence therefore is—as measure, that is, as the "exterior essential form"—the model of the moral action. The concrete moral action is essentially an imitation; it has a constitutive relation to something prior by nature. This something prior by nature to all moral action is the command of prudence. The moral action is not "of itself" good, but it is good because it receives its measure from prudence. The morally good and prudence are—as that which receives the measure and that which provides the measure—identical in their "what." They differ only in their place in the order of realization. The good is the imitation (after-form) of the prudent; the prudent is the original form of the good. The morally good action is the command of prudence, transformed into a new mode of existence.

Prudence as knowledge receives the measure and prudence as command provides the measure. The command of prudence is, as St. Thomas says, a "directing knowledge," *cognitio dirigens.*[9] A commentator on the *Summa Theologica*, the Cardinal Thomas de Vio (Cajetan), speaks of an "active knowing."[10]

The proper and characteristic quality of prudence is the concrete command directed toward willing and acting, but this command is the transformation of previous knowledge. Prudence is the measure of morality, but it first receives its measure from the objective reality of things: "The virtue of the practical reason receives its measure from reality."[11]

And this reception of the measure consists in knowledge being formed by reality. Of this we have spoken enough. "In the *same* way the 'proper mean' in the virtues of the theoretic reason and in those of the practical reason is determined by their conformity to reality."[12] The command of prudence is preceded by its theoretic perceptive identity with objective being.

The question arises upon what areas of reality "prudence as knowledge" turns to receive its measure.

"Prudence applies a general knowledge to particular circumstances."[13] "Therefore it is necessary that the prudent person should know the general basic principles of reason as well as the individual facts with which moral action deals."[14]

The "general basic principles of reason" denotes above all the voice of the primordial conscience, which influences all subsequent partial acts of the whole moral action. The previous voice of the primordial conscience actually makes prudence possible. It works immediately in and with the command of prudence, though not as the most proper and essential element of prudence itself.

Thus, the area of being which belongs properly to "prudence as knowledge" consists of the particular realities and circumstances which "surround" every individual moral action. It is, in a word, the concrete situation of the concrete action, the knowledge of which—besides the natural awareness of the voice of the primordial conscience—is the prerequisite of the command of prudence.

In the command of prudence the knowledge of the concrete situation becomes "directive"; the situation itself, transformed into knowledge and command, turns to the will and imposes an obligation.

Digressions

Three digressions may be necessary here as answers to questions which have probably risen in the mind of the reader; thereby the contour-line of the real purpose of this book will appear more clearly.

First, some readers perhaps expected that we would deal more explicitly with "conscience," but the doctrine of conscience, insofar as it belongs in the context of this investigation, is found not only in our remarks about the primordial conscience but also in our discussion of prudence. Besides and after the primordial conscience *(synderesis)*, the "situation-conscience" *(conscientia)* takes part in the decisive formation of human actions. But the "situation-conscience" which is not, like the primordial conscience, directed to the highest fundamental principles, but to the "application" of these principles, is, when it does not err, prudence itself, insofar as the latter considers, judges and commands rightly.[1]

Therefore, it is not surprising that St. Thomas in his *Summa Theologica* deals specifically with the "situation-conscience" *(conscientia)* in only one article,[2] but with prudence in ten "questions" (fifty-six articles).[3] Moreover, in the reversal of this situation by the newer "Thomistic" moral systems, which hardly speak of prudence but much more of the subjective conscience, we may rightly see a departure from the actual ontological foundation of the ethics of St. Thomas.[4] Secondly, the question of moral obligation and its basis, which is usually bound up with the doctrine of conscience, lies outside the context of this investigation. The basic question of this study of reality and the good concerns the derivation of the "what" of moral commandments from our knowledge of objective reality; the other question concerns not the "what" but the "that," the obligatory quality of the moral imperative. There it is a question of the relation of dependence between the commanding lawgiver and the one commanded; here the question concerns the content and structure of the commandments and their determination by reality.

We do not deny that the superiority of being also affects the question of moral obligation. An absolute and unconditional obligation is only the echo and reflection of an absolute dependence of being. We can speak of unconditional obligation only in the relation of an absolutely independent and an absolutely dependent being, that is, in the relation of God and the creature.

Out of this idea there grows—thirdly—as it were spontaneously, the thought, which must be taken very seriously, whether the reference to the name of God should not have been made more emphatically than we seem to have made it.[5]

In philosophical ethics God may be considered from two points of view: first, as the supreme lawgiver upon whose absoluteness the unconditional nature of moral obligation is based. We have already remarked that, and in what way, this problem lies outside the compass of our present work.

Secondly, God may be considered in philosophical ethics as the creator of man and of the whole finite reality which is related to our knowing and willing as immediately authoritative. Reality has received its measure from God. It is itself the immediate measure of our knowing and willing.

There is a sentence of St. Thomas in which he, perhaps surprisingly, defends himself against the charge of an ethical "short cut," to the absolute. In the *Quaestio disputata* about the cardinal virtues, one "objection" is as follows: the definition of virtue as being according to reason is improper, since reason in turn is subordinate to a higher norm, God himself. Therefore, we must say that the nature of virtue is in this, that it is according to God. To this St. Thomas replies: "The virtues are subordinated to the reason as their nearest or immediate norm, but to God as their ultimate norm. But objects are specified according to their specific and nearest principles, not according to their ultimate principles.[6] Thus, our study of the good as that which is "according to reality" need not press on to the last and absolute norm, provided only that finite reality is not taken to be this absolute norm.

The "positive," revealed, divine law is something different. Its content is immediately fixed by God himself. But in this supernatural sphere the statements of philosophical ethics, if they are true in themselves, remain in force. They are presupposed and receive a new and more valid guarantee. Moreover, in the sphere of the supernatural in which faith receives the "measure" of a new being, which could not be experienced otherwise, it still holds true that the good is that which is according to reality. It is good for man to live and act according to the measure of the reality revealed by God.

Objectivity as an Ethical Attitude

The moral action of man, then, is bound up with reality, with "objects," in this way: The concrete act of the will can be re-translated into the preceding "command" of the practical reason. In their "what" they are identical. The "command" of the practical reason can be re-translated into knowledge. It is nothing but transformed knowledge. Moral action is "doing the truth," *veritatem agere.* The knowledge of the theoretical reason is in the identity of its "what" with the objective world of being, with the "things" from which it receives its "measure." This is an unbroken chain of providing and receiving the measure. Knowledge is reality become subjective, the "command" is directive knowledge, and moral action is a command that has become real.

Objectivity, as the right attitude in knowing, is the fitting answer to the fact that knowledge is essentially determined by reality. Objectivity as an attitude in knowing means that the subject, as subject, refrains from taking any part in determining the content of knowledge.

This attitude on the part of man guarantees true knowledge.

In the ethical sphere "objectivity" means that the attitude of refraining is also extended to all subjective influencing of the "command" and of the action itself, whose content must be determined only by the objective knowledge of reality if a man's action shall be called "good."

It is not necessary to say how much, for instance, the realization of justice among mankind, the supreme and fundamental moral virtue, is directly bound up with "objectivity."

If objectivity in knowledge means recognizing the fact that the content of all knowledge is determined by objects, then in ethics it means further the recognition of the fact that both the interior "command" and the outward action are determined by knowledge. It means that "the attitude of the subject is dictated by the objective *logos*, by the spirit and the *ratio* of the object which he is confronting."[1]

The nature of the practical reason lies in this, that it—first of all in the act of prudence, which is, so to speak, the same thing as "objectivity"[2]—carries out human action by transforming true knowledge into prudent "commands" and prudent "commands" into good actions in relation to the objective reality of "things." To be the passageway for these "things" is the purpose of knowledge and of the "command."

But it would be a mistake to think that by such considerations we would eliminate the subject as subject or degrade it to a mere passageway for objective processes. Cognition, the command, and the exterior action are not "processes" or "occurrences," but acts and deeds of the subject. Without the spontaneous power of the mind and without the impetus of the driving will, none of these acts would ever come to pass. Bringing knowledge, "command" and exterior action into existence, transforming knowledge into "command" and "command" into action—all this is the essentially subjective and basically incomprehensible accomplishment of man, rooted in his personal character and expressing his position in the hierarchy of being, qualitatively superior to all "things."

The thesis that reality is the measure of the good in no way touches or disputes either the originality and individuality of the will or the spontaneity of the subject.[3] Moreover, "objectivity" in knowing is not the same thing as passivity, as we have already stated, and, as an ethical attitude, it is not the same as neutrality, lack of emotion, coldness, indifference. "Objectivity" and passion may well be combined.

The demand for objectivity which we have here—following the "universal teacher" of the Church—derived from the metaphysical nature of human knowledge and action, is found in manifold form in the treasury of wisdom of the human race.

In the book Tao-te-king of Lao-tse we read the truly classical sentence: "He who regards himself does not shine," and again: "To act and take no account of it—that is profound virtue."[4] The sentence of St. Bernard of Clairvaux, which was quoted on the first page of this book, may have been almost a commonplace during the Middle Ages. Three Centuries after Bernard, Thomas à Kempis incorporated it almost verbatim into his *Imitation of Christ*.[5] When people no longer understood the word-play (*sapiens* = wise, from *sapere* = to taste) which underlies the sentence, its content and meaning also seem to have been lost to view. The deep feeling for reality in the mature Goethe re-discovered this meaning. Many of his statements have been incorporated in this book. We shall quote one sentence from his conversations with Eckermann, which deserves special consideration in our voluntaristic times: "Every epoch which is in the process of retrogression and disintegration is subjective, but all progressive epochs have an objective trend."[6]

The idealist ethics of the last century has largely forgotten and denied the determination of morality by reality.

But "ethical realism" receives very significant corroboration from the fact that modern psychology, beginning from an entirely different starting-point, and influenced especially by the discoveries of psychiatry, emphatically declares that "objectivity" is one of the most important prerequisities of psychic health.[7] And we cannot value too highly the significance of this fact: that the inherent therapeutic wisdom of natural psychic and mental life itself reveals the same condition as the basis of health which the ethical and metaphysical consideration of the nature of the created spirit recognizes as the basis of holiness.

Summary

The central concept of the classical-Christian theory of moral action is the concept of the practical reason. This concept mirrors the dependence of moral conduct upon reason and also the dependence of reason upon reality, and thereby the dependence of moral conduct upon reality. In the unity of practical reason and theoretic reason, epistemological realism is united with ethical intellectualism to form an "ethical realism." This twofold relation of the practical reason—to the world of being and to willing and action—represents the metaphysical, ontological basis of classical-Christian ethics.

We shall summarize the result of the preceding study in three statements; the first starts from the concept of the practical reason in general, the second from the practical reason as primordial conscience, the third from the practical reason as prudence.

The practical reason is the measure and the formal cause of morality. At the same time it is essentially one with the theoretic reason, and so is reality of being become the subject. *The measure and formal cause of morality is reality of being become the subject.*

The voice of the primordial conscience is the chief guiding-principle and the natural pre-supposition of morality. It is the practical fundamental principle. At the same time it is the essential structural law of reality, and especially of man himself, which has become directive knowledge.

Therefore, the chief guiding principle and natural presupposition of morality is the basic law of reality and especially of man himself, which has become directive knowledge.

The command of prudence is the immediate measure and formal cause of concrete moral action. At the same time it is the concrete situation of concrete action become directive knowledge. *The immediate measure and formal cause of concrete moral action, therefore, is the concrete situation of concrete action become directive knowledge.*

Conclusion

In the second part of the *Summa Theologica*, in a *question* about the "proper mean," we find an objection which could very easily be passed over but which is the occasion for a statement in which the whole question of *Reality and the Good* is answered succinctly but completely. The objection is as follows: "If the 'proper mean' of moral virtue is determined by intellectual virtue, that is, by prudence, then the proper mean of prudence would, in turn, have to be determined by another virtue, and so we would have an infinite series." St. Thomas replies: "It is not necessary to proceed to infinity in the series of virtues, for the measure and norm of intellectual virtue is not some other virtue, but the thing itself *(ipsa res)*."[1]

Prudence is the measure of the good, but the measure of prudence is not something within the subject, nor yet immediately "God in the conscience," but reality. Prudence determines what is good, but what is prudent is determined by "the thing itself."

Reality, received in knowledge, is not only the first thing given, from which the free will of man begins to move outward toward the world; it is also the final criterion within the world, justifying in retrospect this outward movement.

Appendix

This book is based upon a revision of the author's work *Die Wirklichkeit und das Gute nach Thomas von Aquin* (Münster, 1931 and 1934), which in turn presented a different treatment of an earlier work, *Die ontische Grundlage des Sittlichen nach Thomas von Aquin*, (Münster, 1929).

In the following notes, the quotations from the *Summa Theologica* of St. Thomas Aquinas are marked only by numbers (e.g., II, II, 47, 2 ad 3 refers to the second part of the second section, question 47, article 2, reply to the 3rd objection); the same thing holds true for the quotations from his commentary on the *Sententiae* of Peter Lombard (e.g., I, d.19, 5, 1 equals Book I, distinction 19, question 5, article 1). The titles of the other works of St. Thomas which are quoted in this book are—with the usual abbreviations—as follows: *Summa contra Gentiles* (C. G.), *Quaestiones disputatae de veritate* (Ver.), *Quaestiones disputatae de malo* (Mal.), *Quaestio disputata de virtutibus in communi* (Virt. comm.), *Quaestio disputata de virtutibus cardinalibus* (Virt. Card.), *Quaestiones disputatae de potentia Dei* (Pot.), *De natura verbi intellectus* (Nat. verb. int.), *Quaestiones quodlibetales* (Quol.), *Expositio super S. Pauli epistolam ad Romanos* (Rom.), *Expositio super S. Pauli epistolam ad Colossenses* (Col.).

The statement of St. Bernard of Clairvaux which is prefixed as a motto is found in his *Sermones de diversis* 18, 1; Migne, *Patrologia Latina*, vol. 183, 587. The sentence of Goethe is taken from his "Maximen und Reflexionen," no. 530 (edition of Günther Müller, *Kröners Taschenausgabe*).

Notes

On the Introduction

The Thesis

1. Unumquodque autem intantum perfectum est inquantum est actu; nam potentia sine actu imperfecta est. I, II, 3, 2.
2. Love of oneself is contained in the love of God. I, II, 100, 5 ad 1. Cf. C. G. 3, 22.
3. To Müller, March 28, 1819.
4. Quoted Ver. I, I.
5. De vera religione 36; quoted Ver. I, I.
6. To Schultz, Sept. 18, 1831.

A Realistic Theory of Cognition and Intellectualistic Ethics

1. Intellectus penetrat usque ad rei essentiam; obiectum enim intellectus est "quod quid est." I, II, 31, 5. Omnis cognitio terminatur ad existens. Col. I, 4. Intellectus humani, qui est coniunctus corpori, proprium obiectum est quidditas sive natura in materia corporali existens. I, 84, 7.
2. Voluntas non habet rationem primae regulae; ... dirigitur enim per rationem et intellectum, non solum in nobis sed et in Deo. Ver. 23, 6.
3. Cf. V. Cathrein, "Whether in every sin there is error or ignorance." Gregorianum XI (1930), 553ff.
4. Bonum praesupponit verum. Ver. 21, 3.
5. Bonum per prius pertinet ad rationem sub ratione veri quam ad voluntatem sub ratione appetibilis. I, II, 19, 3 ad 1.
6. Virtus moralis nihil aliud est quam dispositio quaedam seu forma sigillata et impressa in vi appetitiva a ratione. Virt. comm. 9.
7. Ratio est radix omnium virtutum. Virt. comm. 4 ad 3.
8. Bonum hominis est "secundum rationem esse," malum est quod est "praeter rationem." I, II, 18, 5.

9. Primus autem voluntatis actus ex rationis ordinatione non est, sed ex instinctu naturae aut superioris causae. I, II, 17, 5 ad 3.
10. *Ibid.* Also, we must, of necessity, suppose that the will advanced to its first movement in virtue of the instigation of some exterior mover. I, II, 9, 4; cf. also I, II, 9, 6.
11. Cf. for this J. Pieper, *Prudence*, Pantheon (New York, 1959).

On Section I

Reality as the Measure of Cognition

1. Ipsae res sunt causa et mensura scientiae nostrae. Pot. 7, 10 ad 5. Since the speculative intellect is receptive in regard to things, it is in a certain sense moved by things and consequently measured by them. Ver. I, 2.
2. Compare the passages quoted under (1). Also: Our intellect receives knowledge from things, and therefore the cause and measure of truth is the being of the thing itself. Rom. 3, 1.
3. Therefore, all created things are compared to God as products of art to the craftsman. But the craftsman brings his handiwork into being by the ordering of his wisdom and intellect. Therefore, God also made all creatures by the ordering of His intellect. C.G. 2, 24. God made the creature as an agent by intellect and not by a necessity of His nature. C.G. 2, 45. Cf. also C.G. 2, 46 and I, 17, 1.
4. Even in us the cause of one and the same effect is knowledge as directing it, whereby the form of the work is conceived, and will as commanding it, since the form as it is in the intellect only is not determined to exist or not to exist in the effect, except by the will. I, 19, 4 ad 4.
5. C.G. 2, 12.
6. Ver. I, 8.
7. Res naturales, ex quibus intellectus noster scientiam accipit, mensurant intellectum nostrum, sed sunt mensuratae ab intellectu divino, in quo sunt omnia creata sicut omnia artificiata in intellectu artificis. Sic ergo intellectus divinus est mensurans, non

mensuratus; res autem naturalis mensurans et mensurata; sed intellectus noster est mensuratus, non mensurans quidem res naturales, sed artificiales tantum. Ver. I, 2.

8. Intellectus enim humanus est mensuratus a rebus, ut scilicet conceptus hominis non sit verus propter seipsum, sed dicitur verus ex hoc quod consonat rebus. I, II, 93, 1 ad 3.

9. Deus omnium entium est mensura; comparatur igitur Deus ad alia entia, sicut scibile ad scientiam nostram, quod eius mensura est. C. G. 2, 12.

The Identity of Mind and Reality

1. Intellectus in actu et intellectum in actu sunt unum. C.G. 2, 59.

2. Intellectus secundum actum est omnino, id est perfecte, res intellecta. Quod quidem intelligendum est, non quod essentia intellectus fiat res intellecta vel species eius; sed quia complete informatur per speciem rei intellectae, dum eam actu intelligit. Quol. 7, 2.

3. Anima quasi transformata est in rem per speciem. Nat. verb. int.

4. Sciendum est ergo quod in omni intellectu aliqualiter est idem intelligens et intellectum, et in quibusdam aliqualiter differt; in aliqualibus sunt omnino idem. Intellectus enim humanus, qui aliquando est in potentia et aliquando in actu, quando est in potentia intelligens, non est idem cum intelligibili in potentia, quod est aliqua res existens extra animam; sed ad hoc quod sit intelligens in actu oportet quod intelligibile in potentia fiat intelligibile in actu per hoc quod species eius denudatur ab omnibus appendiciis materiae per virtutem intellectus agentis; et oportet quod haec species, quae est intellecta in actu, perficiat intellectum in potentia: ex quorum coniunctione efficitur unum perfectum, quod est intellectus in actu, sicut ex anima et corpore efficitur unum, quod est homo habens operationes humanas. Unde sicut anima non est aliud ab homine, ita intellectum in actu non est aliud ab intellectu intelligente actu, sed idem; non tamen ita, quod species illa fiat substantia intellectus vel pars eius, nisi formalis, sicut nec anima fit corpus. I, d. 35, I, 1 ad 3.

5. "What we assert of things cannot be a mere notion; it is the real things in our imagination." To Riemer, Aug. 2, 1807.
6. Number 1017 (edition Günthur Müller).
7. Intellectus in actu est intellectum in actu propter similitudinem rei intellectae, quae est forma intellectus in actu. I, 87, 1 ad 3.
8. I, 79, 3; 4.
9. Species intelligibilis est similitudo ipsius essentiae rei et est quodammodo ipsa quidditas et natura rei secundum esse intelligibile, non secundum esse naturale, prout est in rebus. Quol. 8, 4.
10. Cf. Ver. I, I.
11. Verum quod est in rebus, convertitur cum ente secundum substantiam. I, 16, 3.
12. Oportet . . . speciem, qua videnda est res, esse "quod quid est" ipsius rei. Caiet. in I, 12, 2.
13. Book III, 429 a.
14. Intellectus autem noster possibilis se habet in ordine intelligibilium sicut materia prima in ordine rerum naturalium. I, 14, 2 ad 3.
15. It follows that sense or intellect is distinct from the sensible or intelligible object, since both are in potentiality. I, 14, 2.
16. Compare the quotation from the commentary on the *Sententiae* under 4; it is clear from the context that here *intellectum in actu* means *species intelligibilis*.
17. Verbum cum re dicta per verbum convenientiam habet maiorem in natura sua quam cum dicente, licet in dicente sit sicut in subiecto. Nat. verb. int.
18. I, 87, 1 ad 3. Also, it is in this sense that we say that the thing actually understood is the intellect in act, because the likeness of the thing understood is the form of the intellect. I, 85, 2 ad 1.
19. Ipsa natura ut existens perfectio rei existentis extra intellectum, recipitur in intellectu, ut est de mente S. Thomae Ver. 2, 2; propter quod dicitur, quod talis natura, puta lapis, perficit intellectum. Quia autem unumquodque est id, quod est, per suam formam et

naturam, ideo sequitur, quod intellectus in actu, ut habet formam et naturam rei intellectae, sit ipsa res intellecta; intelligens enim lapidem est lapis, sicut et habens in se formam lapidis est lapis. Sed tamen, quia forma lapidis non habet esse naturale in intellectu, ex quo habet aliquid, ut absolute dicatur lapis, sed esse intelligibile, intellectus in actu respectu lapidis non dicitur absolute lapis, sed est lapis intelligibiliter. Hic ergo est modus quo intellectus informatus specie alicuius intellecti dicitur ipsum intellectum: quia videlicet habet formam eius per quam est tale. Ferrar. in C.G. I, 44.

20. Erich Przywara, *Ringen der Gegenwart*, Augsburg, 1929, vol. I, 263.

Knowledge and Truth

1. Cognoscentia a non cognoscentibus in hoc distinguuntur, quia non cognoscentia nihil habent nisi formam suam tantum; sed cognoscens natum est habere formam etiam rei alterius. Nam species cogniti est in cognoscente. Unde manifestum est quod natura rei non cognoscentis est magis coarctata et limitata. Natura autem rerum cognoscentium habet maiorem amplitudinem et extensionem. Propter quod dicit Philosophus, quod anima est quodammodo omnia. I, 14, 1; cf. also I, 80, 1 and Ver. 2, 2.
2. Sertillanges, *St. Thomas d'Aquin*, Paris 1910, vol. 2, 105.
3. Intellectus non se habet ut agens vel ut patiens, nisi per accidens; inquantum scilicet ad hoc quod intelligibile uniatur intellectui, requiritur actio vel passio; actio quidem secundum quod intellectus agens facit species esse intelligibilis actu; passio autem secundum quod intellectus possibilis recipit species intelligibiles. . . . Sed hoc quod est intelligere, consequitur ad hanc passionem vel actionem sicut effectus ad causam. Ver. 8, 6.
4. . . . only if there is something which is such that it agrees with every being. Such a being is the soul, which as is said in *The Soul* "in some way is all things." Ver. I, 1.
5. In ipsa operatione intellectus . . . completur relatio adaequationis, in qua consistit ratio veritatis. I, d. 19, 5, 1.

Objectivity as an Attitude in Knowing

1. Cf. J. Pieper, "*Wirklichkeitswissenschaftliche*" *Soziologie. Kritische Randbemerkungen zu Hans Freyer, "Soziologie als Wirklichkeitswissenschaft.*" Archiv für Sozialwissenschaft und Sozialpolitik, vol. 66, 394-407.
2. Cf. Ver. 10, 8 and I, 87, 3.
3. Nullus percipit se intelligere nisi ex hoc quod aliquid intelligit: quia prius est intelligere aliquid quam intelligere se intelligere. . . . Intellectus . . . non est intelligibilis nisi per speciem superinductam. . . . Mens nostra non potest seipsum intelligere ita, quod seipsam immediate apprehendat; sed ex hoc quod apprehendit alia, devenit in quam cognitionem. Ver. 10, 8.

On Section II

The Unity of Theoretical and Practical Reason

1. I, 79, 11, sed contra.
2. Intellectus enim practicus veritatem cognoscit sicut speculativus, sed veritatem cognitam ordinat ad opus. I, 79, 11 ad 2.
3. The speculative and practical intellects are not distinct powers. The reason of which is that what is accidental to the nature of the object of a power does not differentiate that power. . . . Now, to a thing apprehended by the intellect, it is accidental whether it be directed to operation or not, and according to this the speculative and practical intellects differ. For it is the speculative intellect which directs what it apprehends, not to operation, but to the consideration of truth; while the practical intellect is that which directs what it apprehends to operation. I, 79, 11.
4. *Grundlegung zur Metaphysik der Sitten*, Introduction.
5. *Ibid*, Conclusion.
6. Richard Kroner, *Von Kant zu Hegel.* Tübingen, 1921/24. Vol. I, 153.
7. I, 79, 11, sed contra.
8. 3, d. 23, 2, 3, 2.
9. I, d. 27, 2, 1.

The Structure of Moral Action

1. 3, d. 17, 1, 2, 1.
2. St. Thomas did not present moral action from a single point of view. As far as the cognitive partial acts are concerned, he presented them in part under the aspect of the *habitus* supporting them, e.g., *synderesis* and *prudentia;* or else he takes individual partial acts and gives a detailed phenomenological description, e.g., in the case of *consilium* and *imperium; consilium, iudicium* and *imperium* he combines under the concept of the virtue of prudence; the act of *synderesis* he considers both from the point of view of its supporting *habitus* and from the point of view of its content, which is the natural moral law.
3. Bonum habet rationem finis. I, 5, 2 ad 2.
4. In ordine autem agibilium primo quidem oportet sumere apprehensionem finis. I, II, 15, 3.
5. I, II, 19, 3 ad 1.
6. In unoquoque autem horum appetituum amor dicitur illud quod est principium motus tendentis in finem amatum. I, II, 26, 1.
7. The curious word *synderesis* is the Greek συντέρησις [=preservation]; the Latin form can be explained by the medieval Greek pronunciation. In the translation of the *Summa Theologica* by Joseph Bernhart, *synderesis* is translated by "Gewissensurschatz" (primitive store of conscience). This rather felicitous rendering is, however, deficient in that it expresses rather the content of the primordial conscience than this conscience itself.
8. There is in the soul a natural habit of first principles of action, which are the universal principles of the natural law. This habit pertains to synderesis. Ver. 16, 1.
9. The act of the natural habit called *synderesis* is to warn against evil and to incline to good. Ver. 16, 1 ad 12.
10. The act of the will is to will, to choose and to intend. It is to will in so far as reason proposes to the will something good absolutely. . . . It is to intend in so far as reason proposes to the will a good as an end to be attained through a means. Ver. 22, 15. Cf. also I, II, 12, 2.
11. Sunt autem quattuor actus rationis, secundum quod dirigit

humanos actus: quorum primus est intellectus quidam, quo aliquis recte existimat de fine, qui est sicut principium in operativis. . . . Secundus actus est consilium de agendis. Mal. 14, 4.

It is tempting to interpret the *recte existimare de fine*, which here appears as the "first act" of the reason "insofar as it directs human actions," as the voice of the primordial conscience. But we must consider that *existimare* does not imply an imperative but rather a theoretical evaluation.

12. Since counsel is an inquiry, it is not of the end but only of the means. I, II, 14, 2.

13. The application of the appetitive movement to counsel's decision is consent properly speaking. I, II, 15, 3.

14. All thought about those things of which counsel takes cognizance is directed to the formation of a right judgment, wherefore this thought is perfected in judgment. II, II, 53, 4 ad 2. Also: Tertius actus est iudicium de agendis. Mal. 15, 4. Compare the passage quoted under 11.

15. A decision or judgment, to be followed by choice. I, II, 13, 1 ad 2.

16. Choice is the taking of one thing in preference to another. I, II, 13, 2.

17. Sed si inveniatur unum solum quod placeat, non differunt re consensus et electio. I, II, 15, 3 ad 3.

18. Not every act of the will precedes this act of the reason which is command; but an act of the will precedes, viz. choice, and an act of the will follows, viz. use. Because after counsel's decision, which is reason's judgment, the will chooses; and after choice the reason commands that power which has to do what was chosen, and then, last of all, someone's will comes to use, by executing the command of reason. I, II, 17, 3 ad 1.

19. Now there are three acts of reason in respect to anything done by man: the first of these is counsel, the second judgment, the third command. . . . The third is proper to the practical intellect, in so far as this is ordained to operation. I, II, 57, 6.

20. I, II, 16, 4.

21. The extension of the reason to include willing, which takes place in the succession of the cognitive partial acts, is, however, not a simple progressive movement of the practical element in them. The practical element in the reason, in the course of the cognitive partial acts, reaches, so to speak, two climaxes, one in the voice of the primordial conscience, the other in the "command" of prudence. These two acts constitute "climaxes" of the practical element because both are imperatives. The voice of the primordial conscience is a general and abstract imperative, the "command" of prudence a definite and concrete one. The voice of the primordial conscience is preceded by the purely theoretic acts of cognition, between the voice of the primordial conscience and the concrete "command" lie the more theoretical acts of "consideration" and "judgment."

22. Ratio apprehendit aliquid in universali, sed appetitus tendit in res quae habent esse particulare. I, II, 66, 3.

23. *Synderesis* does not mean the rational power simply but as perfected by a completely determined habit. Ver. 16, 2 ad 4.

24. As a result, for probity to be possible in human actions, there must be some permanent principle which has unwavering integrity, in reference to which all human works are examined, so that that permanent principle will resist all evil and assent to all good. This is synderesis, whose task it is to warn against evil and incline to good. Therefore, we agree that there can be no error in it. Ver. 16, 2.

25. Just as in the operative part of the soul synderesis never errs, so in the speculative part understanding of principles never errs. Ver. 16, 1.

26. Sicut non contingit in speculativis intellectum errare circa cognitionem primorum principiorum, quin semper repugnet omni ei quod contra principia dicitur, ita etiam non contingit errare in practicis in principiis primis; et propter hoc dicitur quod synderesis extingui non potest. 2, d. 39, 3, 1.

27. Ad prudentiam pertinet recte consiliare, iudicare et praecipere de his per quae pervenitur ad debitum finem. II, II, 47, 10.

The Voice of the Primordial Conscience

1. *Synderesis* is said to be the law of our mind, because it is a habit containing the precepts of the natural law. I, II, 94, 1 ad 2. The natural law is contained primarily in the eternal law, but secondarily in the natural code of the human reason. I, II, 71, 6 ad 4. The precepts of the natural law are to the practical reason what the first principles of demonstrations are to the speculative reason. I, II, 94, 2.

2. Oportet quod prima directio actuum nostrorum ad finem fiat per legem naturalem. I, II, 91, 2 ad 2. Also: The first rule of reason is the natural law. I, II, 95, 2. Not conscience, but synderesis is the first rule of human activity. Ver. 17, 2 ad 7. Natural reason, known by the name of synderesis, appoints the end to moral virtues. II, II, 47, 6 ad 1.

3. The first principle in the practical reason is one founded on the notion of good. I, II, 94, 2.

4. There is no act ascribed to synderesis which cannot be performed by reason. Ver. 16, 1. The natural law is something appointed by reason. I, II, 94, 1.

5. Sicut enuntiatio est rationis dictamen per modum enuntiandi, ita lex per modum praecipiendi. I, II, 92, 2.

6. Bonum est quod omnia appetunt. Ver. 21, 1.

7. In itself it might be possible to take the voice of the primordial conscience, if it is considered in isolation, as a purely indicative statement: *bonum est faciendum*, the good "is" that which should be. O. Renz in his comprehensive work on synderesis in Thomas Aquinas (Münster, 1911), at least in the chapter on the "evidence" of the synderesis judgment (p. 70), almost completely disregarded its dynamic, imperative character. The judgment of the synderesis, says Renz, is "objectively evident" because in it subject and predicate are identical. But this way of looking at things is possible and meaningful only in pure indicative statements. The judgment of the synderesis, however, is not "the good 'is' that which should be," but "the good 'should be.'" The same thing is expressed in the fact that St. Thomas calls the content of the synderesis-judgment "the natural *law*."

8. Et ideo primum principium in ratione practica est quod fundatur supra rationem boni, quae est "bonum est quod omnia appetunt." Hoc est ergo primum praeceptum legis, quod bonum est faciendum et prosequendum, et malum vitandum. I, II, 94, 2.

9. It follows that the very fact that the reason moves by commanding is due to the power of the will. I, II, 17, 1. A form considered by the intellect neither moves nor causes anything except through the medium of the will, whose object is an end and a good by which one is moved to act. C.G. 1, 72.

10. Secundum ordinem inclinationum naturalium est ordo praeceptorum legis naturalis. I, II, 94, 2.

11. Intention is an act of the will in regard to the end. Now the will stands in a threefold relation to the end. First, absolutely; and thus we have volition. . . . Secondly, it considers the end as its place of rest; and thus enjoyment regards the end. Thirdly, it considers the end as the term toward which something is ordained; and thus intention regards the end. For when we speak of intending to have health, we mean not only that we will have it, but that we will have it by means of something else. I, II, 12, 1 ad 4. Intention regards the end as a terminus of the movement of the will. I, II, 12, 2.

12. This dependence of prudence upon the will, however, is of a very different kind from the dependence of the external action of the will upon the "command" of prudence. Here it is not a matter of likeness and reciprocity. The dependence of the will upon the reason concerns the "what" of willing and action, just as the dependence of the reason upon reality concerns the "what" of thinking. But the "command" of prudence does not receive its "what" through the rightness of the will, but the rightness of the preceding act of the will makes it possible that the "command" of prudence receive its "what" from true knowledge. Therefore, P. Th. Deman, O.P., is mistaken in his criticism of the first edition of this book. Cf. *Revue des sciences philosophiques et théologiques*, 19, 718 ff.

13. II, II, 47, 13 ad 2.

14. I, II, 15, 3.

15. I, II, 90, 1 ad 3.

16. Actus cognitionis praeexigitur ad actum ipsius *(synderesis)*. Ver. 16, 1 ad 14. This touches upon the fact that the primordial conscience is an innate *habitus:* An act of knowing is not prerequisite for the power or habit of sÿnderesis, but only for its act. Hence, this does not prevent the habit of synderesis from being innate. *Ibid.*

17. Praecipere quod est applicare cognition habitam ad appetendum et operandum. II, II, 47, 16.

18. Ver. 16, 1, obj. 14 ad 14.

19. I, II, 94, 2.

20. Here we are not dealing with the question how the reason—considered psychologically—attains the concept of the good; whether it is formed, as Cathrein thinks, spontaneously from the natural inclination of the subject. Nor are we concerned with the problem whether the objective presuppositions which are included in the concept of the good are fulfilled consciously and actually and controllably in the intellect.

21. Omnia appetunt suam prefectionem. I, 5, 1.

22. But goodness signifies perfection which is desirable and consequently of ultimate perfection. Hence, that which has ultimate perfection is said to be simply good. I, 5, 1 ad 1. Good has not only the character of the perfect but also that of the perfective. Ver. 21, 3 ad 2.

23. Perfectionis nomen, si stricte accipiatur, in Deo non potest poni, quia nihil est perfectum nisi quod est factum. Ver. 2, 3 ad 13.

24. Unumquodque tantum habet de bono quantum habet de esse. I, II, 18, 1.

25. The good or evil of an action, as of other things, depends on its fullness of being or its lack of that fullness. I, II, 18, 2.

26. I, 48, 1.

27. Quia vero bonum habet rationem finis, malum autem rationem contrarii, inde est quod omnia illa, ad quae homo habet naturalem inclinationem, ratio naturaliter apprehendit ut bona et per consequens ut opere prosequenda, et contraria eorum ut mala et vitanda. I, II, 94, 2.

28. We may recall here the passage quoted under 10.

29. Lex naturalis nihil aliud est quam participatio legis aeternae in rationali creatura. I, II, 91, 2.

30. Lex aeterna nihil aliud est quam ratio divinae sapientiae, secundum quod est directiva omnium actuum et motionum. I, II, 93, 1.

31. I, II, 91, 1.

32. . . . if the natural law were something different from the eternal law; whereas it is nothing but a participation thereof. I, II, 91, 2 ad 1.

33. Cf. J. Mausbach, *Katholische Moraltheologie.* Münster, 1918-1922. Vol. 1, 55.

34. I, II, 91, 2.

35. Virtutes perficiunt nos ad prosequendum debito modo inclinationes naturales, quae pertinent ad ius naturale. II, II, 108, 2.

Prudence

1. Cf. for this whole section J. Pieper, *Traktat über die Klugheit.*
2. "Psychological" and "moral" considerations of the primordial conscience therefore coincide. Hence, there can be no objection to including the act of the primordial conscience in the "processus psychologique de l'acte humain." Cf. the review of the first two editions of this book by Odon Lottin, *Recherches de Théologie ancienne et médiévale* I, 61* and 4, 543*.

3. . . . prudentiam, secundum id quod est cognoscitiva, . . . secundum quod est praeceptiva. II, II, 48.

4. The truth of practical intellectual virtue . . . in relation to the appetite has the character of a rule and measure. I, II, 64, 3.

5. Ad ea, circa quae ratio operatur, se habet ut regula et mensura; ad ea vero, quae speculatur, se habet ratio sicut mensuratum et regulatum ad regulam et mensuram. Virt. comm. 13.

6. Idem ergo est medium prudentiae et virtutis moralis; sed prudentiae est sicut imprimentis, virtutis moralis sicut impressi;

sicut eadem est rectitudo artis ut rectificantis et artificiati ut rectificati. Virt. comm. 13.

7. All the other moral virtues . . . are formed through prudence as by a proximate form. Ver. 14, 5 ad 11. Prudence supplies the form in all other moral virtues. 3, d. 27, 2, 4, 3.
8. The rectitude of reason is the mean of moral virtue and also the mean of prudence—of prudence as ruling and measuring, of moral virtue as ruled and measured by that mean. I, II, 64, 3. Cf. also the sentence quoted under 6.
9. Virt. card. 1.
10. Notitia activa, qualis convenit prudentiae. Caiet. in I, II, 57, 4.
11. Verum autem virtutis intellectualis practicae, comparatum quidem ad rem, habet rationem mensurati. I, II, 64, 3.
12. Eodem modo accipitur medium per conformitatem ad rem in virtutibus intellectualibus practicis sicut in speculativis. I, II, 64, 3.
13. Prudentia applicat universalem cognitionem ad particularia. II, II, 49, 1 ad 1.
14. To prudence belongs not only the consideration of the reason but also the application to action, which is the end of the practical reason. But no man can conveniently apply one thing to another unless he knows both the thing to be applied and the thing to which it has to be applied. Now actions are in singular matters; and so it is necessary for the prudent man to know both the universal principles of reason and the singulars about which actions are concerned. II, II, 47, 3.

Digressions

1. "La conscience droite et certaine n'est autre qu'un acte de la prudence, qui conseille, qui juge pratiquement et qui commande, "Garrigou-Lagrange, *Du caractère métaphysique de la théologie morale de St. Thomas, en particulier dans ses rapports avec la prudence et la conscience. Revue thomiste*, 8. Cf. also B. H. Merkelbach, *Summa theologiae moralis.* Paris, 1932, Vol. 2, 42.
2. I, 79, 13.

3. II, II, 47-56.

4. This reproach is expressed, e.g., quite plainly by Garrigou-Lagrange in the article referred to under 1.

5. Cf. the review of the first edition of this book in *Divus Thomas* (Freiburg, Switzerland) 9, 100 ff.

6. Virtutes morales attingunt rationem sicut regulam proximam, Deum autem sicut regulam primam. Res autem specificantur secundum propria et proxima principia, non secundum principia prima. Virt. card. 1 ad 10.

Objectivity as an Ethical Attitude

1. D. v. Hildebrand, *Die neue Sachlichkeit und das katholische Ethos.* Der Katholische Gedanke 4 (1931).

2. The concept of prudence emphasizes more the relation to willing and action, the concept of objectivity stresses more the relation to reality.

3. Cf. the reviews of the first editions of this book in the *Revue Bénedictine*, 44, 84 ff., in the *Revue des sciences philosophiques et theologiques*, 19, 718 ff. and 20, 791 ff., in the *Bulletin Thomiste* 9, 529 ff., in the *International Journal of Ethics*, 42.

4. Ch. 24 and 51. In the translation of Viktor von Strauss and Torney.

5. Bk. 2, ch. 1, 31.

6. Jan. 29, 1826.

7. Cf. J. Pieper, *Sachlichkeit und Klugheit. Über das Verhältnis von moderner Charakterologie und thomistischer Ethik.* Der Katholische Gedanke 5 (1932).

Conclusion.

1. Non est necesse in infinitum procedere in virtutibus; quia mensura et regula intellectualis virtutis non est aliquod aliud genus virtutis, sed ipsa res. I, II, 64, 3 ad 2.

The Structure of Moral Action.
(cf. p. 55)

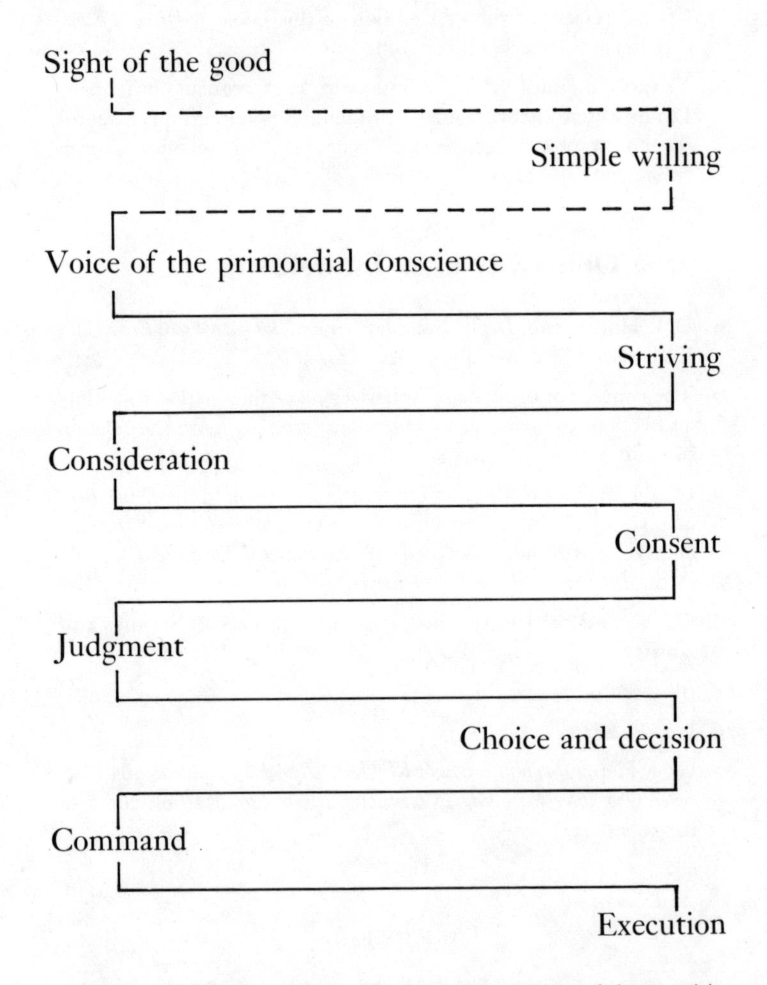

[The left side of this diagram shows the succession of the cognitive partial acts, the right side that of the volitional.]